Make Your Own Playdough, Paint, and Other Craft Materials

Make Your Own Playdough, Paint, and Other Craft Materials

Easy Recipes to Use with Young Children

Patricia Caskey

Redleaf Press
www.redleafpress.org
800-423-8309

Published by Redleaf Press
10 Yorkton Court
St. Paul, MN 55117
www.redleafpress.org

First edition 2006
Cover illustrations by Patrice Barton
Interior typeset in Full Moon by Bitstream and designed by Liz Tufte, Folio Bookworks
Interior illustrations by Patrice Barton
Printed in the United States of America
15 14 13 12 11 10 09 08   2 3 4 5 6 7 8 9

Library of Congress Cataloging-in-Publication Data
Caskey, Patricia.
    Make your own playdough, paint, and other craft materials : easy recipes to use with young children / Patricia Caskey.
        p. cm.
    ISBN 978-1-933653-05-1
1. Handicraft—Equipment and supplies. 2. Artists' materials—Formulae. I. Title.

    TT153.7.C37 2006
    745.5028′4—dc22   2006012906

Printed on acid-free paper

Make Your Own Playdough, Paint, and Other Craft Materials

77 Chapter 4: Paste & Glue Recipes

87 Chapter 5: Goop & Glop Recipes

141 Chapter 7: Discovery Bottles

149 Chapter 8: Discovery Table Ideas

Acknowledgments

Thank you to all who supported and encouraged my efforts. I want to especially thank my mom and dad for always being there for me—no matter what. Thank you to Lori and Kim for always keeping a smile on my face. The biggest thanks goes to all the children who were my "scientists" and "recipe testers" over the years. They are the inspiration that made this book possible.

Visit my Web site for more ideas to use in the classroom or at home! The Chalkboard is located on the World Wide Web at www.kidschalkboard.com.

Web site hosting provided by www.posisites.com, a subsidiary of Positier Technologies.

Thank you very much, and I hope you enjoy all the craft recipes!

Introduction

Through a child's eyes, the simplest of things are often wondrous. The world is a vast arena of learning, full of magnificent discoveries. I wrote this book with that in mind. All craft recipes involve some kind of discovery. The process of combining ingredients and seeing the end result of something made with their own hands can be both exciting and empowering for young children. Children enjoy the sensory experience they get from rolling, smashing, poking, and prodding. When they mold clay, manipulate playdough, or paint a picture, children make sense of their world. The recipes in this book can be made at home or in the classroom, by you alone or with the children. Regardless of who makes the recipes and why, at every step in the process, children will learn and explore, and most important, have fun!

Why Make Your Own Craft Materials?

Almost ten years ago I began teaching four-year-old preschoolers. Working in a Head Start program, I found that money was not always readily available for classroom supplies. This is when I began making my own playdough. Not only did making my own playdough save me money, but making it was so much easier than I ever imagined. I began by looking around and collecting a variety of dough and paint recipes and making them with the children in my classroom. The children enjoyed the process of generating their own art supplies. It didn't matter to them that the supplies weren't store-bought. The children just wanted to play.

Making your own craft materials has a number of advantages. The majority of recipes that follow can be made with ingredients already found in your kitchen. Oftentimes flour, salt, water, and a few other ingredients are all you need to fill the afternoon with creative play. Because the ingredients are so readily available, the craft materials you can make using these recipes are often cheaper than those you might find in a store.

In addition to being simple and inexpensive, making your own craft materials gives children the opportunity to be involved in the process of creating, which has endless possibilities for learning and playing. Children can help you measure and mix, cut and bake. This can be empowering to children, and they will learn about science, math, reading, and art in the process.

Making your own craft materials also gives you the flexibility that many store-bought products don't. Many of the recipes in this book can be altered by adding scented oils and spices, paint or food coloring. Some of the paints can be changed by adding textures, such as cornmeal, sand, or corn syrup. Don't feel limited by the specific ingredients labeled in each recipe. By adding to the main ingredients, you may end up with something new and exciting! If it doesn't turn out, that's okay! Just try again! That's what discovery is all about!

What Children Learn—Making the Connection

Who would think that something as simple as making playdough could promote so much learning in children? There are tremendous opportunities for learning and exploring in the mixing and measuring, the cutting and baking. When you read the recipes with the children, or make a shopping list, you promote early literacy skills. They develop math skills when they measure the ingredients or compare the sizes and shapes of the different products. Making your own craft materials fosters science skills when the children learn to observe and predict. When they see all the ways they can change the shape of the clay, or how it changes when they put it in the oven, children gain a better understanding of the physical world. When they manipulate and roll the playdough with their hands, they strengthen their fine motor skills, which is essential to early writing. Finally, in the process of creating, molding, and painting, the children cultivate their artistic and creative abilities.

Though much of this learning will happen naturally in the course of children's play, there are certain things you as a parent or provider can do to enhance it. Their thinking skills expand when you ask them questions about what will happen next, or why things happened the way they did. Sharing and cooperation skills develop in children when you advise them to wait their turn with the paint or encourage them to share the playdough with their peers.

Perhaps the most important thing children will accomplish while making their own craft materials is the sense of pride that comes from creating something new. The sense of accomplishment is so much greater when children create a pinch pot from a simple mixture of flour, salt, and water than if they just open a premixed package. In addition, a child learns much more by making the clay himself and then molding it into a vase. The experience is even more special when the vase is given to a loved one, knowing it was made—start to finish—with the child's own two hands.

Promoting Creativity

Creativity is a process. As children create, they make many decisions. They decide what to paint, sculpt, or write. They decide which colors they will use, which way to move their art utensil or pencil, and when their artwork is complete. If they encounter a difficulty in the process, they must determine how to overcome it. Children learn to think and solve problems in creative ways by making mistakes and learning from them. Their solutions and decisions are an integral part of the creative process.

As a teacher, child care provider, or parent, you can do a variety of things to help keep a child's creative juices flowing. For example, you can do the following:

- Avoid closed-ended projects. Creative art isn't a row of ducks that all have the same colors, shapes, and designs. Having children use their imaginations to make their own vision of a turkey out of clay is much more child-centered. Closed-ended projects have a useful purpose, but open-ended projects promote much more creativity.

- Offer a variety of materials and opportunities to use them. Children can't use their imagination much with only one color of crayon or one color of paper. Provide an assortment of paints for children to mix to produce different colors. Provide the opportunities for cutting and pasting, writing and coloring, and painting and stenciling.

- Give children freedom. This doesn't mean allowing the children to paint the walls! Encourage creative thinking and individuality. As adults, we see the sky as blue and the grass as green. When children paint, they might decide to paint a yellow sky or purple grass. It is important not to stifle children's creativity by correcting them. They probably know the color of the sky and the grass, but it is through this experimentation process that they inspire creativity in themselves. By giving children instructions that are too specific or by making an exact model for them to copy, you inadvertently stifle that creativity. Children tend to want to mimic grown-up behavior and may become frustrated when their flower isn't the same as yours.

- Provide a special area for children to express themselves. Have you ever tried to draw with a crayon on a piece of paper on the carpet? It isn't an easy task, and it's hard to be creative when you're frustrated. Provide a hard surface for painting, rolling dough and clay, and drawing. The children will appreciate it and will be able to work much more easily.

- Provide encouragement and support. Children benefit greatly from encouraging words. Rather than saying, "That's beautiful," use descriptive words to describe their efforts. Statements such as "I like all the colors you used in your rainbow" or "That is very smart of you to add a sun to the sky" not only support their efforts, but also show children you are truly looking at their work.

Safety

Craft recipes may seem harmless enough, but there are various matters to take into account when making your own clays and paints with young children.

One of the most obvious concerns is keeping young children away from a hot stove. Never leave a child alone near an open flame or hot oven. Recipes that call for boiling or baking should be done with adult supervision. Even better, adults should complete these steps themselves.

The majority of the recipes are nontoxic. All the recipes have been tested by a chemist for safety and by professional child care providers for effectiveness. There are, however, several recipes that include ingredients that could be toxic if ingested in large quantities. Some of these ingredients are listed below. Take extra precautions when using these ingredients with children:

Alum: Do not ingest.

Borax: Do not ingest. Could also be a topical irritant.

Essential oils: Do not ingest.

Glycerin: Do not ingest in large quantities.

Liquid starch: Do not ingest in large quantities.

Orrisroot powder: Do not ingest.

Perfume: Do not ingest.

Rubbing alcohol: Do not ingest. Could also be a topical irritant.

Shaving cream: Do not ingest.

Soap or liquid detergent: Do not ingest.

Vinegar: Do not ingest in large quantities.

These ingredients, as well as any others that should not be ingested, are marked with a star in each recipe. Children should be supervised closely by an adult when using any of these ingredients.

All of the recipes have specific age recommendations, as some are not suitable for babies and toddlers. The age range can vary greatly, however, depending on a child's developmental level. Some of the recipes labeled for older children can be used with younger children if they are supervised closely. Follow your own judgment and an individual child's developmental level.

Take all these safety concerns into consideration when creating any of these recipes. Be safe!

How to Use This Book

This book includes eight chapters covering a range of different craft recipes from playdough to paint, bubbles to chalk. At the beginning of each chapter you will find a list of the different ways you can use the products, as well as a list of all the skills children will develop as they work with the materials. At the end of each chapter there is a section of craft projects you can use with the recipes. Each project contains a suggested list of recipes that work best for the project. I hope you use these projects as a starting point in creating your own activities. Don't feel tied down by any of the recipes or projects. Being inventive is just as important for the adult as it is for the child! Experiment and discover new ways of mixing, new and different ingredients to add, new ways of using them, etc. Of course, you will need to use caution and not add ingredients that are toxic, either by themselves or in combination with other materials.

Creativity and discovery go hand in hand. The job of adults is to help children discover new creative outlets. I hope you and the children around you enjoy making and using these recipes as much as I have!

Happy creating!

Playdough

1

You can . . .

- manipulate it into various forms and shapes
- cut it with scissors
- poke, cut, and scoop it with various utensils
- use cookie cutters and rollers
- press hands and feet or objects into it to make impressions
- add glitter or food coloring
- roll onto a pegboard, fly swatter, or screen
- air-dry or bake to make ornaments
- add fragrant oils or spices

Children will be . . .

- using language to discuss the look, feel, smell, and touch of the dough
- learning math by measuring
- strengthening hand and finger muscles
- learning about science by adding too much or too little of something
- increasing hand-eye coordination
- using their imagination and cultivating creativity
- predicting and comparing

This recipe is great for young hands. Suitable for all ages with supervision while using a hot stove.

Cooked Playdough

- ⅓ cup cornstarch
- 1½ cups water
- 3 tablespoons talcum powder*
- 3 tablespoons liquid dish soap*
- 2–3 drops food coloring

Put the cornstarch in a medium saucepan. Add water to the pan a little at a time; stir until water and cornstarch are mixed. Cook the mixture over low to medium heat until it comes to a boil and thickens, stirring continuously (about 6–8 minutes). Remove from heat. Add talcum powder and soap and stir until mixed. Divide into equal portions. Place the dough in a bowl and mix with food coloring for color.

* Do not ingest.

This is the easiest playdough to make and it's easily pliable for young hands. This dough doesn't last as long as cooked dough, but it can be stored for about a month in an airtight container. Suitable for all ages with supervision.

No-Cook Playdough

- 1 cup flour
- 1/3 cup salt
- 1/2 cup water or as needed
- 2–3 drops food coloring
- 4–5 drops liquid detergent*

Mix the flour and salt together in a bowl. In a separate bowl, mix the water, food coloring, and detergent. Slowly add this mixture to the flour and salt. Knead well on a flat surface and shape into a ball.

* Do not ingest.

This dough has a pleasant scent and texture. Suitable for all ages with supervision.

Potpourri Dough

- 1 cup flour
- $\frac{1}{2}$ cup salt
- 1 cup potpourri*
- $\frac{1}{2}$ cup water

Mix together the flour, salt, and potpourri. Gradually add water until the dough holds together. Mold or cut into desired shapes. Air-dry to harden.

* Do not ingest.

This dough is stiffer than regular playdough. Use it to make small sculptures, photo holders, or vases. Supervision is required due to the use of a hot stove. Suitable for all ages.

Ceramic Dough

- 2 cups salt
- $^2/_3$ cup water
- 1 cup cornstarch
- $^1/_2$ cup cold water

Mix the salt and $^2/_3$ cup water in a pan. Heat the mixture, stirring until the salt is thoroughly dissolved. Remove from heat. Mix the cornstarch and $^1/_2$ cup cold water in a separate bowl. Stir quickly into the first mixture and mix thoroughly.

The following two doughs are great for adding any scent you desire. Use scents that convey the different seasons or holidays. Supervision is required while using boiling water. Suitable for all ages.

Scented Dough

- 2 cups flour
- 1 cup salt
- 4 teaspoons cream of tartar
- 2 tablespoons vegetable oil
- 2–3 drops scent (vanilla extract, peppermint, lemon, etc.)
- 2 cups water
- 2 packages unsweetened drink mix

Mix the flour, salt, cream of tartar, vegetable oil, and scent in a bowl and put aside. Boil 2 cups of water and add the unsweetened drink mix. Mix everything together thoroughly. Knead the mixture when it is cool enough to handle. Air-dry to harden.

This recipe is a treat for the senses. Add any scent you want, or break the dough up into sections and use a number of different scents for an exciting sensory experience. Suitable for all ages.

Another Scented Dough

- 3 cups flour
- 1 cup vegetable oil
- 2–3 drops scent (vanilla extract, peppermint, lemon, etc.)
- 2–3 drops food coloring (optional)
- $\frac{1}{2}$ cup water

Combine the flour, oil, scent, and optional food coloring. Add water until the dough is easily manipulated.

This is a wonderful dough to use around the holidays. Use with holiday cookie cutters or shape into a festive sculpture. The scent will fade a bit when dried. Suitable for all ages.

Cinnamon Dough

- 2 cups flour
- 1 cup salt
- 5 teaspoons cinnamon
- 3/4–1 cup water

Mix dry ingredients together in a bowl. Pour the water into the bowl and mix with your hands until the dough forms a solid mass. (More flour or water may be added if the dough is either too sticky or too crumbly.) Knead the dough on a board until smooth.

Use this dough to make festive ornaments around the holidays. Suitable for all ages with supervision.

Cinnamon Dough for Ornaments

- 1½ cups ground cinnamon
- 1 cup applesauce
- ¼ cup white school glue*
- water, if needed

Mix the cinnamon, applesauce, and glue together in a bowl. The dough should be as thick as cookie dough. Add a bit of water if it is too stiff. Remove the dough from the bowl and knead. Place the dough back in the bowl, cover with plastic wrap, and let sit about an hour. Remove the dough and knead it again to make it smooth. Flatten the dough on a piece of waxed paper until it is about ¼-inch thick. Cut out desired shapes and use a straw to punch a hole for a ribbon to hang the ornament with later. Place the ornaments between two sheets of waxed paper and dry for 3–5 days. Turn them over a few times a day to dry and to reflatten.

* Do not ingest.

Use this dough to hide treasures in, and when hardened, break it open for a fun surprise! This dough can be used to incorporate a lesson on geodes, or to play a guessing game. It also makes a unique gift idea. Suitable for all ages with supervision.

Surprise Treasure Dough

- 1 cup flour
- 1 cup used coffee grinds
- ½ cup salt
- ¼ cup sand*
- 1 cup water

Mix all the dry ingredients together. Slowly add the water to make a stiff dough. Knead on a floured surface until smooth. Break into desired "rock" sizes. Hide toys and surprises in the center of each ball of dough. Allow the dough to dry for 3–4 days. Break open the "rocks" for the surprise inside.

* Do not ingest.

This dough is similar to clay, but easier to manipulate. Use it to make small sculptures, photo holders, or garden stones. See the craft projects at the end of this chapter for additional ideas. Suitable for ages 3 and up due to the use of alum. Alum can be purchased at any science supply store.

Clay Dough

- 3 cups flour
- 3 cups salt
- 3 tablespoons alum*
- 2–2¹/₂ cups water

Combine all the dry ingredients and slowly add water, a little at a time. Mix well with a spoon. As the mixture thickens, continue mixing with your hands until it has the feel of clay. If it's too dry, add water. If it's too sticky, add equal parts flour and salt.

* Do not ingest.

This dough is a bit more rubbery than the previous dough and provides for a great sensory experience. Use it to make a paperweight or a stand for a small object, or just have fun playing with it. Suitable for all ages, with supervision around the hot stove.

Salt Dough

- 1 cup salt
- 1 cup water
- ½ cup flour

Mix the ingredients together in a pot and cook over medium heat. Remove from heat when the mixture is thick and rubbery. As it cools, knead in any additional flour to make a usable dough.

This dough will remind you of the winter holidays! Use cookie cutters to make holiday shapes or create ornaments in the shape of gingerbread people. See the end of this chapter for hints on how to make these and other projects.

You can substitute pumpkin pie spice for the cinnamon and add orange food coloring to make pumpkin pie spice dough. Suitable for all ages.

Gingerbread Dough

- 2 cups flour
- 1 cup salt
- 2 tablespoons ground cinnamon
- 1 tablespoon ground cloves
- 1 cup water

Mix all the dry ingredients together. Add water gradually. Knead the dough until smooth.

This dough is a variation of the previous recipe. Use it to make ornaments, cut it into shapes, or just have fun manipulating it and taking in the scent. Suitable for all ages.

Another Gingerbread Dough

- 1 cup flour
- 1/2 cup salt
- 2 teaspoons cream of tartar
- 1/2 cup cinnamon and allspice, combined
- 1 cup water
- 4 drops food coloring (equal parts red and green)
- 1 teaspoon vegetable oil

Mix the dry ingredients together in a bowl. Add more cinnamon and allspice to your liking. In a separate bowl, add the food coloring to the water. Add this mixture along with the vegetable oil to the dry ingredients and stir. Pour the mixture into a pot and cook for 2–3 minutes, stirring often. Allow to cool and then knead.

This dough is a bit unusual. You don't manipulate it as you would normal dough. Instead you bake it into various shapes and decorate when cooled. Take care to supervise younger children around a hot stove.

Cotton Puff Dough

- 1 cup flour
- 1 cup water
- 1 bag cotton balls*

Mix flour and water together to make a paste. Add the cotton balls to the paste and mix thoroughly. Scoop out small amounts of the dough, allowing excess paste to drop away from the cotton balls. Form the dough into desired shapes on a baking sheet. Bake for 1 hour at 325 degrees. This dough can be painted when cooled.

* Do not ingest.

This dough is specifically designed to be baked in desired shapes. Air-drying may cause it to crack. Use this dough to make vases, photo holders, or small sculptures. Suitable for all ages with supervision while using a hot stove.

Baking Dough

- 2 cups flour
- 1 cup salt
- 1 cup water

Mix enough water with the flour and salt to form a dough. Cut into desired shapes and bake at 300 degrees for about 1 hour to harden.

This dough dries very hard and is not easily broken and is therefore good for making objects and figurines. Suitable for ages 3 and up due to the use of sawdust.

Sawdust Dough

- 2 cups sawdust*
- 3 cups flour
- 1 cup salt
- 2 tablespoons water or as needed

Combine all the ingredients, adding water as needed. Air-dry to harden.

* Do not ingest.

This recipe uses natural fruit juices to add exciting new colors to your dough. Suitable for all ages.

Nature's Playdough

- 1 cup flour
- 1/2 cup salt
- 2 tablespoons cream of tartar
- 2 tablespoons vegetable oil
- 1 cup water
- 2 tablespoons beet, spinach, or carrot juice

Mix the flour, salt, cream of tartar, and oil and slowly add water. Cook over medium heat and stir until stiff. Turn onto waxed paper and cool. Divide into balls. Add the vegetable juice to make pink, green, or orange dough. If you don't have these vegetable juices on hand, simply puree the vegetable in a blender and pour off the liquid.

This recipe is good for making stepping stones or flower pots. Suitable for all ages.

Bumpy Texture Dough

- ¾ cup flour
- ¼ cup salt
- 2–3 tablespoons water

Mix the flour and salt, and add the water. Mix with your hands to form a dough.

You can use this dough to make bird feeders or to just play. It smells delicious! Suitable for all ages.

Peanut Butter Dough

- 1 cup peanut butter
- 1 cup white corn syrup
- 1 cup powdered sugar
- 3 cups powdered milk

In a bowl, mix the peanut butter, corn syrup, and powdered sugar. Add the powdered milk and knead until smooth.

This dough is easily made by children with their own hands, and it tastes great! The texture of this dough is a little bit more sticky than the others. Suitable for all ages.

Frosting Dough

- 1 can prepared frosting, any flavor
- 1½ cups powdered sugar
- 1 cup peanut butter

Mix all the ingredients in a bowl. Knead into a workable dough.

This dough is very similar to the peanut butter dough, but varies slightly in texture. Toddlers can mix it themselves and lick their fingers too! Suitable for all ages.

Honey Dough

- 1 cup powdered milk
- ½ cup creamy peanut butter
- ½ cup honey

Mix together all the ingredients. Coating your hands with butter will prevent some of the stickiness.

Creative Craft Projects Using Playdough

Paperweight

For use with ceramic dough, salt dough, or bumpy texture dough

Shape the dough into desired size. Embellish by pressing objects into the dough, scraping designs into the dough, or adding art gems or glitter. If you want to paint it, do so after it has dried.

Garden stone

For use with clay dough

Coat any container or shaped mold that has fairly deep sides with petroleum jelly or cooking spray. Pie or bread tins work well. Make sure sides are as deep as you would like your stone's thickness to be. Press the dough into the desired mold. If you want to embellish your stones with objects, place the objects in the form before adding dough. Allow to dry 3–4 days. Pop stone out of mold. Paint if desired. Apply polyurethane (adults only, taking proper precautions) to prevent weathering.

Photo holder

Different clays and doughs will result in different textures and/or scents for this project. Use ceramic dough, clay dough, salt dough, or baking dough if you want to paint the holder or add embellishments. If you want texture, use salt dough, sawdust dough, or bumpy texture dough. Use potpourri dough, the scented doughs, cinnamon dough, or gingerbread dough for scented holders.

The photo holder can display several photos, which will hang from curved pipe-cleaners that are set in a playdough base.

To make the base, form the dough into whatever shape you'd like, making sure the bottom is flat. It will need to stand on a level surface. Insert the pipe cleaners into the base so they stand upright. These will hold the photos. Curl the tops of the pipe cleaners about 1 inch down, enough to slip a small ribbon over. Punch holes in the tops of the photos, loop ribbons through, and hang one photo on each pipe cleaner. The photo holder can also be used to hang small seasonal or holiday ornaments.

Stand for a special object

Make a display for a favorite object, such as a special rock or any small item. For use with ceramic dough, clay dough, salt dough, sawdust dough, or nature's playdough.

To make the stand, form the dough into a solid base, making sure the bottom is flat so it will stand on a level surface. Carefully carve out a small hollow in the base to fit the object you want to display. The object should sit nicely on top of it. Dry the dough according to the recipe you use. Paint if desired.

Bird feeders
For use with peanut butter dough or honey dough

Form the peanut butter or honey dough into medium-sized balls. Insert a string through the center of the balls and tie a knot on one end. Roll the dough in birdseed until it is coated. Hang the bird feeder from a tree and watch the birds flock to it!

Vase
For use with baking dough

This recipe is great for making vases. Take a large lump of dough and shape it into whatever shape of vase you want. Use your imagination! Make sure the bottom is flat, and then dry according to the recipe directions. When it is dry, thickly spread glue over the entire vase. Starting at the top, slowly wind some thick twine around the vase, wrapping it all the way around until you reach the bottom. Let dry 48 hours.

Wrapped candy decorations
For use with clay dough or cotton puff dough

Form the dough into small, round, disklike shapes. Allow to dry. When they are dry, wrap the disks with colored cellophane. Tie each end so that the wrapped disks resemble pieces of hard candy. Use them to decorate photo frames, small pinch pots, etc.

ClaY

2

You can . . .

- press the clay into a mold and allow it to dry
- make pinch pots, vases, bowls, sculptures, or paperweights
- make refrigerator magnets or ornaments for gifts
- make jewelry, trivets, coasters, or tiles
- add texture using Popsicle sticks, forks, or paper clips
- make impressions in the clay using bolts, seeds, paper clips, or yarn
- use on a pottery wheel
- make handprint keepsakes

Children will be . . .

- enhancing their fine motor skills
- developing hand-eye coordination
- increasing their vocabulary and language skills as they talk about the clay
- cultivating their creativity
- using their senses
- enhancing their social skills
- learning math by making patterns on the pinch pots or bowls
- engaging in dramatic play with characters made out of clay

This clay resembles wet sand. It's great for making pretend sand castles. You can also cut it into fun shapes using summer-themed cookie cutters. Suitable for all ages with supervision using the hot stove.

Sand Clay

- 1 cup cornstarch
- 2 cups sifted sand
- 1 1/2 cups water

Mix all the ingredients together. In an old pot, cook over medium heat for 5–10 minutes until the mixture leaves the sides of the pot. (Note: The sand may scratch the surface of the pot, so use a pot that you don't mind ruining.) Cool the clay, knead, and store.

Baker's clay is great for sculpting bowls, pinch pots, and other items that would normally require a kiln. It does best when it is baked, but can be air-dried if desired. Suitable for all ages with supervision while using a hot stove.

Baker's Clay

- 4 cups flour
- 1 cup salt
- 1½ cups water
- 2–3 drops food coloring
- liquid tempera paint* and varnish* (optional)

Mix all the ingredients together. To harden, shape and air-dry for about 48 hours, or bake in a 250 degree oven for about 1 hour. After it hardens, paint or decorate, and then varnish.

* Do not ingest.

Like the previous recipe, this clay can be used to make pinch pots, bowls, or small sculptures. See the end of this chapter for hints on how to make these and other projects. This recipe is suitable for all ages with supervision while using the hot stove.

Another Baker's Clay

- 1 cup cornstarch
- 2 cups baking soda
- 1½ cups cold water

Combine all the ingredients. Stir until smooth. Cook the mixture over medium heat until it reaches the consistency of dry mashed potatoes. Turn the clay onto a plate, covering with a damp cloth. When the clay is cool enough to handle, knead it on a surface covered with cornstarch until it is smooth. Store in a plastic bag.

Little fingers will find this clay very easy to manipulate. It's great for exploring and shaping. Suitable for all ages, using supervision with the hot stove.

Play Clay

- ½ cup salt
- ½ cup hot water
- ½ cup cold water
- ½ cup cornstarch

Mix the salt and hot water in a pot, and bring the mixture to a boil. In a separate bowl, mix the cold water and the cornstarch. Add the cornstarch mixture to the boiling water and stir. Cook over low heat, stirring constantly. When the mixture is smooth, remove from the heat and cool. Knead into a ball. To store this clay, wrap it in foil and refrigerate.

This clay is special because if it is hardened in the sun, it won't crack! Use it to make pinch pots or handprint keepsakes. Suitable for all ages with supervision while using the hot stove.

Sun Clay

- 2 cups salt
- $^2/_3$ cup water
- 1 cup cornstarch
- $^1/_2$ cup water

Place the salt in a pot and add $^2/_3$ cup water. Stir and cook over medium heat for 4–5 minutes until the salt is dissolved. Remove from the heat. In a separate container, gradually mix $^1/_2$ cup water with 1 cup cornstarch. Stir until smooth and add to the salt mixture. Knead and shape.

This clay is a good use for stale bread that would otherwise get thrown away. Suitable for ages 3 and up with adult supervision.

NOTE: This recipe contains detergent or glycerin, which may be harmful if ingested. This dough is not edible.

Bread Clay

- 6 slices white bread
- 1 tablespoon white school glue*
- 1/2 teaspoon liquid detergent or 2 teaspoons glycerin*
- 1/2 tablespoon water
- 2–3 drops food coloring (optional)

Remove the crusts from the bread and discard them. Knead the bread and the white glue in a bowl. Add the detergent or glycerin and the water. Knead until the mixture is no longer sticky. Add more water if the clay is too crumbly and dry. Separate into portions and add a few drops of food coloring if desired. Mold into any shape. To harden, dry overnight. For a glossy coat and a smoother appearance, brush with equal parts of glue and water.

* Do not ingest.

And you thought dryer lint wasn't good for anything! Paint or decorate this clay to your desire or use it as you would papier-mâché. Suitable for ages 3 and up with adult supervision while using the hot stove.

Dryer Lint Clay

- 1¹/₂ cups dryer lint*
- 1 cup water
- ¹/₂ cup flour
- 2 drops wintergreen mint flavoring
- liquid tempera paint* (if desired)

Place the lint in a saucepan and cover it with the water. When the lint is saturated, add the flour and stir until smooth. Add the drops of wintergreen mint flavoring. Cook the mixture on low heat, stirring constantly, until it forms peaks and holds together. Pour it onto newspaper to cool. To harden, air-dry 3–5 days. Do not dry in a stove because of fire hazards. Once dry, paint if desired.

* Do not ingest.

This recipe is great for toddlers to make their own beads and practice stringing them all by themselves. You can also use it to make necklaces and bracelets. Suitable for all ages.

Clay Jewelry Mixture

- ³/₄ cup flour
- ¹/₂ cup cornstarch
- ¹/₂ cup salt
- 1 tablespoon warm water or as needed
- liquid tempera paint* (if desired)

Mix together the flour, cornstarch, and salt. Add water gradually until the mixture can be kneaded to reduce stickiness. The mixture may be rolled into balls to make beads. Poke a hole in each bead with a toothpick or large needle and allow to dry. The beads can then be painted and put on a string.

* Do not ingest.

In this recipe, you will make small balls of clay containing a little bit of food coloring in the center. When the clay is manipulated, it changes color! Younger children love this recipe. Have the children guess what color their balls of clay will be inside, or squish balls of different colors together and discuss color mixing. Suitable for all ages with supervision while using the stove.

Surprise Soda Clay

- 1 cup baking soda
- 1/2 cup cornstarch
- 3/4 cup water
- 2–3 drops food coloring

In a saucepan, stir together the baking soda and cornstarch. Add water and mix well over low heat, stirring occasionally for 7–8 minutes. Remove the pan from the heat and allow the mixture to cool. When cool, turn onto a board coated with cornstarch and knead into a workable clay. Separate into 4–6 balls. Make a small well in each ball and add a few drops of food coloring. Seal the well by pinching the clay closed (don't let the color seep out the sides).

Children can make their own closet deodorizers with this recipe! Add it to sock drawers or use it as a car air freshener. This clay makes any number of great gift ideas. Suitable for ages 3 and up. Take care that the orrisroot and essential oil are not ingested. Orrisroot can be found at any store that sells herbs or other natural supplements.

Herbal Clay

- 1/3 cup pulverized dry herb (lavender, comfrey, etc.)
- 1 tablespoon orrisroot powder*
- 1/4 cup flour
- 5–10 drops of essential oil*
- 2–3 tablespoons water
- 2–3 drops food coloring (optional)

Mix all ingredients in bowl except the water. Add 2–3 tablespoons of water to the dry mix. If mixture is too dry, add more water, a little at a time. If it is too wet, add more dry mix. Add food coloring if desired. Form into the desired shape and lay to dry. After a while the scent may dissipate. If it does, add a few drops of essential oil to the dry surface to refresh.

* Do not ingest.

Children love this recipe because it's edible. Make your creation, then devour it! (Make sure you work on a clean surface and that the children wash their hands before playing with the dough!) This dough can be stored for up to a week if wrapped tightly. Suitable for all ages.

Candy Clay

- ⅓ cup margarine
- ⅓ cup corn syrup
- ½ tablespoon salt
- 1-pound box powdered sugar
- 2–3 drops food coloring

Mix all the ingredients together and mold into any shape you want.

Creative Craft Projects Using Clay

Seasonal tree stand

For use with sand clay, any baker's clay, or sun clay

Press a ball of clay into the bottom of any small container. Insert a small branch into the clay so that the branch stands upright, and allow the clay to dry. You can decorate the outside of the container with glued-on paper or paint. In addition, try hanging any seasonal or holiday items from the branches. For added beauty, leave about an inch of space from the clay to the top of the container and cover this surface with colored sand.

Handprint keepsake

For use with baker's clay or sun clay

Take a large clump of clay and form it into the desired shape for the handprint base. Make sure clay is fairly thick. Press the child's hand into the clay. Use a pencil or an old pen and carve out the child's name and the date in the clay. To create a hanging keepsake, use a straw to add a hole near the top of the base for a ribbon. Dry according to the instructions in the recipe you used.

Pinch pot
For use with any baker's clay, bread clay, or herbal clay

Roll the clay into a small ball. Poke a thumb hole into center of ball. Pinch opening wider and wider to form a small pot. Embellish your pinch pot by pressing small objects into the clay and removing them, leaving an impression. Dry according to instructions in the recipe you used. Then, if desired, paint using poster paint.

Beads
For use with clay jewelry mixture

Roll the clay into small balls and mold into the desired shapes for beads. Push a hole through the center of each bead using a nail or, for a bigger hole, a straw. Decorate beads by rolling them in glitter, pressing in art gems, or allowing them to dry and then painting them. When dry, place the beads on a string to create jewelry, or use the beads for a patterning or in a fine motor skills activity.

Pebble pot
For use with sand clay, any baker's clay, or sun clay

Mold a lump of clay into a large round shape about 3 inches in diameter. Flatten one side to form a base and carefully cut the clay in half horizontally. The top half will be the lid, and the bottom half will be the pot. Hollow out the inside of the bottom half, leaving sides that are fairly thick. Let the pot harden, and then paint.

Holiday ornaments
For use with any baker's clay

Roll the clay flat so that it is about 1/2-inch thick. Cut it into fun shapes using cookie cutters. Use a straw to make a hole in the top of each shape for a ribbon. Bake the clay as instructed to dry, and add ribbon. This clay can be colored with markers or painted.

Candy canes
For use with any baker's clay, play clay, or sun clay

Take two lumps of clay and color each with either red or green food coloring, or leave one white. Roll each lump in your palms to form a rope. Then twist the two ropes together to form one intertwined rope. Smooth the ends. Bend into a cane shape, and dry according to instructions.

Clay photo transfer
For use with baker's clay

For this project, you will transfer a favorite photo or image onto a piece of clay! It's best to use white clay for this project. Roll out a ball of clay so that the surface is big enough to frame a picture. Print a desired photo or picture from your computer onto T-shirt transfer paper, which can be found at any craft store. Cut out the photo and lay it on the clay and smooth the surface. Make sure the whole surface is touching the clay; otherwise, it won't print. Place the clay into the oven, with the paper still attached. Bake at 250 degrees for 5–7 minutes. Take out and carefully remove the paper. Place the clay back into the oven and complete the baking according to the instructions in the recipe. Let cool in the oven.

Paint

3

You can . . .

- paint on a variety of surfaces such as sandpaper, cardboard, posterboard, paper, foil, waxed paper, or fabric
- paint with different tools such as paintbrushes, toothbrushes, or squeeze bottles
- spatter paint or blow paint onto paper
- create ink blots by dripping paint onto a paper and folding it in half
- use your fingers to paint
- add fragrance or spices to the paint for scented paint
- add salt, crushed leaves, or glitter for a different texture
- make a shadow painting by placing an object or cutout onto the paper and painting around it

Children will be . . .

- using language to discuss the look, feel, smell, and touch of the paint
- learning math by measuring ingredients
- expanding their creativity
- using their senses
- learning about colors and color mixing
- using vocabulary when describing the process of painting
- learning science by exploring texture
- enhancing their visual acuity

Face and body paint can be costly. This recipe isn't! Apply this paint with cosmetic sponges, cotton swabs, or small brushes. This recipe will last for up to a month if stored in an airtight container. Keep it out of eyes and mouths. Please use caution and note any allergies children may have to lotions or paints. This recipe is suitable for ages 3 and up.

White Face Paint

- 2 teaspoons white liquid tempera paint*
- 1 teaspoon cool water
- 1/2 teaspoon white hand lotion*
- 1/2 teaspoon colored powdered tempera paint* (optional)

In a small paper cup, mix all the ingredients together by stirring. Add a few drops of water if mixture is too thick. To add color to the face makeup, mix in powdered tempera paint, or use another color of liquid tempera paint as the base.

* Do not ingest.

This is another recipe for face paint that can be used for Halloween costumes, playing dress-up, or any other way you can imagine. Apply this paint with cosmetic sponges, cotton swabs, or small brushes. Keep out of eyes and mouths. Please use caution and note any allergies children may have to any of the ingredients. This paint should last for up to a month if stored in an airtight container. Suitable for ages 3 and up.

Face Paint

-  4 tablespoons shortening
- 2 teaspoons cornstarch
- 2–4 teaspoons liquid tempera paint*

Mix ingredients together well. This recipe makes enough for one color.

* Do not ingest.

Yet another recipe for body paint! Recycle those used film canisters to store the different colors. This paint should last up to a month if stored in an airtight container. Use caution and watch for any allergies children may have to any of the ingredients. Suitable for ages 3 and up.

Body Paint

- 1 cup baby lotion*
- 1 tablespoon liquid dish soap*
- 1 teaspoon powdered tempera paint*

Mix the ingredients together. Add a few drops of water if the mixture is too thick.

* Do not ingest.

This recipe makes a lovely, sparkly paint, and it's a lot less messy than pouring glitter onto paper. Suitable for all ages with supervision.

Glitter Paint

- ½ cup white school glue*
- 3 teaspoons liquid tempera paint*
- 3 teaspoons glitter*

Mix all ingredients together.

* Do not ingest.

This paint dries to a beautiful, shiny finish. Suitable for ages 3 and up due to the use of liquid starch. Be careful that this is not ingested.

Dazzling Tempera Paint

- 2 cups powdered tempera paint*
- 1 cup liquid dish soap*
- 1 cup liquid starch*

Mix the paint and soap. Add starch and stir. Add more soap if the paint is too thick.

* Do not ingest.

This paint is like liquid sidewalk chalk! Use it to draw pictures or write messages on the sidewalk. It washes off with ease! Suitable for all ages.

Sidewalk Paint

- ¹/₄ cup cornstarch
- ¹/₄ cup cold water
- 6–8 drops food coloring

Mix the cornstarch and cold water in a small bowl. Add the food coloring and stir.

This paint will make the room smell great. It's fun to mix and easy to clean up. Suitable for ages 3 and up.

Shaving Cream Paint

- 1 can white shaving cream*
- Powdered or liquid tempera paint* as needed

Sprinkle or squirt paint onto pile of shaving cream. Mix with hands.

* Do not ingest.

This paint is fun to make. Use your fingers to paint with it, or brush it on heavy paper. Suitable for all ages.

Whipped Cream Paint

- 8-ounce container whipped cream
- 2–3 drops each of different colors of food coloring

Mix the food coloring and whipped cream together to make desired color.

The following two recipes can be used to paint cookies, cakes, breads, and other baked goods. Use either before or after baking to add a nice pattern or a fun picture to your baked goods. The egg paint will add a light, crispy texture. Suitable for all ages with supervision while using the raw eggs.

Egg Paint

🥄 2–3 drops food coloring
🥚 2 egg yolks*

Mix food coloring with egg yolks using a fork.

* Do not ingest..

Use this paint to add a fun face or another colorful design to slices of bread. Nontoxic and suitable for all ages.

Paint for Bread

-  1 tablespoon milk
- 1 drop food coloring
- bread slices

Mix the milk and food coloring together and paint it on slices of bread using a cotton swab or a clean paintbrush.

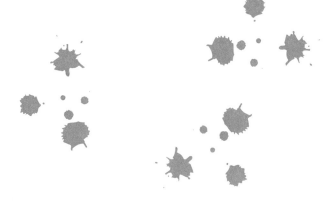

This "paint" is slightly different from the others in that it's powdered! Make a picture using glue and sprinkle this paint over the paper like you would glitter. This paint can also be used to make beautiful colored sand jars. Suitable for all ages with supervision.

Sand Paint

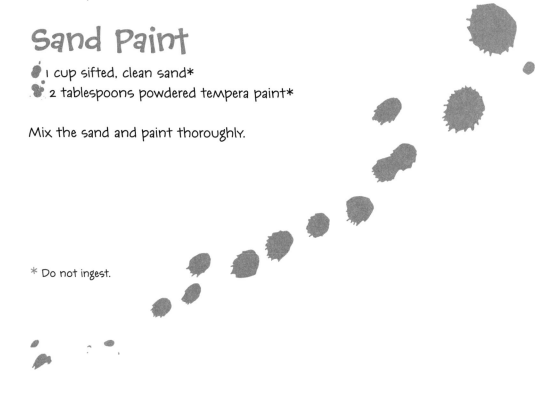

- 1 cup sifted, clean sand*
- 2 tablespoons powdered tempera paint*

Mix the sand and paint thoroughly.

* Do not ingest.

Use this paint to add a little texture to your artwork. This paint is great for making ocean murals! Suitable for ages 3 and up due to the use of liquid starch. Use caution and be careful that the children do not ingest this.

Salt Paint

- 2 teaspoons salt
- 1 teaspoon liquid starch*
- 1 small container liquid tempera paint*

Mix salt and starch into the paint. You can also add just the salt to the paint, but you will have to use a lot of it if you do not use the starch.

* Do not ingest.

As good as the paint you can buy in a store, and a lot cheaper! This paint takes a little longer to make than the others, but it is worth the time. Store it in an airtight container in the refrigerator to extend its life. Suitable for all ages with supervision while using the hot stove.

Fingerpaint

- 1 packet unflavored gelatin
- 2½ cups cold water, divided
- 1 cup cornstarch
- ½ cup soap flakes*
- 2 drops icing color paste (available at craft and baking supply stores)

In a small bowl, add the gelatin to ½ cup of water and mix until dissolved. Separately combine the cornstarch, soap flakes, and remaining 2 cups of water in a saucepan over medium heat. Add the gelatin mixture to the saucepan, stirring until it becomes thick. Remove the pan from the heat and strain the mixture equally into 4 containers. Cool 1 hour and then add a different shade of icing color paste to each container. Fold in the color until thoroughly mixed. Store in the refrigerator.

* Do not ingest.

This is a simple fingerpaint that you mix as you go. Suitable for ages 3 and up due to the use of liquid starch. Be careful that the children do not ingest this.

NOTE: Undiluted color paste will stain hands and clothing.

Easy Fingerpaint

- 1 tablespoon liquid starch*
- 1 teaspoon powdered tempera paint*
- 1 teaspoon water

Pour a small amount of starch onto a piece of paper. Sprinkle a teaspoon of paint into the starch. Add water as needed, mixing with the hands while painting.

* Do not ingest.

This fingerpaint is fun to play with because it's sticky!
Suitable for all ages.

Sticky Fingerpaint

- 1 tablespoon light corn syrup
- 2–3 drops food coloring

Pour corn syrup onto a paper plate. Squirt food coloring into the puddle. Mix with fingers, and paint.

This paint is very thick and good for using on regular paper. Suitable for all ages with supervision while using the hot stove.

Cornstarch Fingerpaint

- 5 teaspoons cornstarch
- 4 cups cold water
- 2–3 drops food coloring

Mix the cornstarch with a small amount of water. Gradually add all the water to the mixture. Cook over low to medium heat until the paint is clear and thick as pudding. Add food coloring.

NOTE: This paint may stain hands and clothing, so wear an apron or old clothes while you prepare it.

Once it's prepared, you don't have to worry about cleanup! Suitable for all ages with supervision.

No-Mess Fingerpaint

- ½ cup clear hair gel*
- 2–3 drops food coloring
- sealable plastic bag

Put the food coloring and hair gel into the sealable bag. Make sure bag is sealed well (otherwise it will no longer be a no-mess recipe). Lay the bag flat and, keeping it sealed, allow the children to use their fingers to draw colorful shapes on the bag. Then, simply press to erase!

* Do not ingest.

This paint is easy to clean up and smells great too! Suitable for ages 3 and up with supervision around the hot stove. Be careful that this is not ingested.

Soap Flakes Fingerpaint

- 1½ cups dry laundry starch*
- 1 tablespoon cold water
- 1 quart boiling water
- 1½ cups soap flakes*
- 2–3 drops food coloring

Mix the starch with cold water (enough to make a paste). Add boiling water and stir until clear. Cool and add the soap flakes and food coloring. Store in sealed containers.

* Do not ingest.

Children love this paint. Use it to paint masterpieces in the bathtub! It makes bathtime fun! Suitable for all ages with supervision while using the hot stove.

Bathtub Fingerpaint

- ⅓ cup cornstarch
- 1½ cups water
- 3 tablespoons talcum powder*
- 3 tablespoons mild liquid dish soap*
- 2–3 drops food coloring

Put the cornstarch in a saucepan. Add water a little bit at a time. Stir until mixed. Cook over low to medium heat to a boil until thickened. Stir continuously for approximately 6-8 minutes. Remove from heat. Add talcum powder and soap. Stir until mixed. Divide the paint, and color with food coloring.

* Do not ingest.

This recipe is great for toddlers to make with your help. It stimulates the senses. Suitable for all ages with supervision while using the paint.

Scratch-and-Sniff Paint

2–3 drops flavoring extract, or as desired
liquid tempera paint*

Add flavoring extract to the paint. Use any liquid extract you desire. Allow to dry. Scratch and sniff!

* Do not ingest.

This is another simple fingerpaint that children can make on their own. It smells great and has a gooey consistency. Suitable for all ages with supervision.

Glue Paint

- ¼ cup white school glue*
- 3–4 drops food coloring, or as desired

Pour the glue into a bowl. Add food coloring. The more food coloring you add, the darker the paint. Mix thoroughly. Repeat for as many different colors as you'd like.

* Do not ingest.

Watercolors can be expensive. This recipe is a wonderful alternative! This is also a good recipe to use to explain the science behind why the ingredients fizz when combined. (When vinegar and baking soda are combined, carbon dioxide is released!) Suitable for all ages with supervision.

Homemade Watercolors

- 1 tablespoon clear vinegar*
- 1 tablespoon baking soda
- 1 tablespoon cornstarch
- ½ teaspoon corn syrup
- 2–3 drops food coloring

Mix together the vinegar and baking soda. When the fizzing stops, add the cornstarch and the corn syrup. Add food coloring to create the color you want.

* Do not ingest.

Here's another paint you can lick your fingers clean with! This paint is great for toddlers. Suitable for all ages with supervision while using the hot stove.

Pudding "Paint"

- 1 package pudding mix
- waxed paper

Cook pudding mix according to directions. Pour ¼ cup onto waxed paper. Allow children to make designs with their fingers. They love to lick their fingers after painting.

This is a great recipe for younger children, and the children can lick their fingers along the way! This paint is best squeezed from a squeeze bottle. It takes up to 2 days to dry. Suitable for all ages.

Package Cake Mix "Paint"

- 1 package cake mix
- 1 cup water, or as specified on cake package
- 1/3 cup vegetable oil, or as specified on cake package
- 2–3 drops food coloring (if desired)

Follow directions on package, but omit the eggs. Divide batter into squeeze bottles and tint with food coloring if desired. Children can squeeze their paint onto heavy paper or cardboard.

Creative Craft Projects Using Paint

Foldovers

For use with dazzling tempera or any paint other than the face paints

Fold a piece of colored construction paper in half. Drip small puddles of paint onto one side of the paper. Fold paper closed and smash down until flat. Carefully open the paper and look at your design!

Fruit/vegetable print

For use with dazzling tempera or any paint other than the face paints

Cut any piece of fruit or vegetable in half. Dip the fruit or vegetable, flat side down, into paint. Press onto paper.

Color mixing

For use with any of the paints in this chapter

Use any of the paint recipes to mix and create new colors. Mix yellows and blues to make greens, yellows and reds to make oranges, blues and reds to make purples. Experiment to make the colors brown and black.

Painting on different surfaces

For use with glitter paint, dazzling tempera paint, shaving cream paint, sand paint, salt paint, cornstarch fingerpaint, glue paint, or homemade watercolors

Paint on a variety of surfaces: paper, cardboard, waxed paper, foil, tissue paper, coffee filters, plastic, or glass.

Painting with different tools

For use with any of the paints in this chapter

Paint with rollers, toothbrushes, sponges, cotton swabs, bark, marbles, feathers, combs, cotton balls, eyedroppers, etc.

Absorption painting

For use with homemade watercolors, glitter paint, and dazzling tempera paint

Dip a small corner of a coffee filter into any thin, watery paint. Watch as the coffee filter absorbs the paint. Dip it into various colors to create different effects.

Ocean painting

For use with salt paint

Add blue and green food coloring to salt paint to make a painting or mural of the ocean.

Yarn or string painting

For use with glitter paint, dazzling tempera paint, or homemade watercolors

Take a piece of yarn or string, about 6 inches long, and dip it into the paint until it is saturated. Drag the yarn or string across a piece of paper.

Marble painting

For use with glitter paint or dazzling tempera paint

Place a piece of paper into a deep-sided lid of a pot or jar. In separate dishes, pour paint colors and add a few marbles. Pick up marbles with a spoon or fingers and drop them onto the lid. Tilt the lid until the paper is streaked with the paint. Add a new color. Continue until you reach the desired effect.

Bubble wrap painting

For use with dazzling tempera paint or glitter paint

Dip a piece of bubble wrap into paint and then press onto a piece of paper. Explore different colors and patterns. This makes a pretty wrapping paper!

Reverse painting

For use with any of the paints used in this chapter

Take a cutout of any shape and place it on a piece of white paper. Paint over the entire paper. When dry, remove the shape and you are left with a nice silhouette!

Tin can painting

For use with any of the paints used in this chapter

Wind a piece of twine around a tin can, spiraling around the can from the top to the bottom. Tie the string in place. Roll the can in paint so the string picks up the color. Roll the can on paper.

Blow painting

For use with dazzling tempera paint

Drop a large glob of paint onto paper. Take a straw and, keeping it an inch above the paper, blow the paint across the paper.

Paste & Glue

4

You can . . .

- make magazine collages
- make greeting cards for special occasions
- decoupage furniture
- make tissue-paper stained-glass pictures
- bind homemade books
- make a texture collage using Styrofoam, tissue, or fabric
- make your own stickers or labels
- use to glue macaroni, rice, or beans onto paper

Children will be . . .

- enhancing eye-hand coordination by cutting, tearing, and gluing
- learning about the properties of glue
- learning science by experimenting
- learning math by measuring

The cornstarch in this recipe thickens the mixture into a nice paste. Store this glue in an airtight container. Suitable for ages 3 and up due to the use of alum. Supervise while using the hot stove.

Cornstarch Paste

- ¼ teaspoon alum* (can be purchased at a science supply store)
- 1 tablespoon flour
- 2 tablespoons cornstarch
- 2 tablespoons cold water

Mix the alum, flour, and cornstarch together. Slowly add the water, stirring to get rid of any lumps. Cook in a double boiler over low heat, stirring constantly. When the paste begins to thicken, remove it from the heat. The mixture will continue to thicken after it has been removed. If necessary, thin the paste with water.

* Do not ingest.

This glue is a very simple, watered-down glue that doesn't leave creases like regular glue. It's great for making collages. Keep this glue in an airtight container. It may need to be shaken occasionally to prevent separation. Suitable for all ages with supervision.

Collage Glue

- 3 parts white school glue*
- 1 part warm water

Combine the glue with water in a jar or a bottle with screw-on lid. Shake until well mixed. Brush a thin layer on paper and smooth out.

* Do not ingest.

This is the best glue for binding cloth to cardboard to make notebooks and scrapbooks. It can also be used to bind leather to leather. See the craft projects at the end of this chapter for bookmaking tips. Suitable for ages 3 and up due to the use of glycerin. Make sure children do not ingest it.

Bookbinding Glue

- 1 packet unflavored gelatin mix
- 3 tablespoons boiling water
- 1 tablespoon vinegar*
- 1 tablespoon glycerin*

Add the gelatin to the boiling water. Stir until dissolved. Add the vinegar and glycerin. Stir until well mixed. Makes about $1/3$ cup.

* Do not ingest.

This glue is great for sealing jars or other craft projects that involve glass containers. It doesn't keep long unless you add oil of cloves as a preservative. Suitable for all ages with supervision while using the hot stove.

Waterproof Glue

- 2 packets unflavored gelatin mix
- 2 tablespoons cold water
- 3 tablespoons skim milk
- several drops oil of cloves* (optional)

In a small bowl, sprinkle the gelatin mixture over cold water. Set aside to soften. Heat milk to boiling point and pour into softened gelatin. Stir until gelatin is dissolved. While the glue is still warm, brush a thin layer on the objects to be glued. To store, add oil of cloves and place in a jar. If the glue hardens after storing it for a while, you can set the jar in a pan of hot water to soften glue for reuse.

* Do not ingest.

Glue in the hands of young children goes quickly. This glue resembles regular school glue, so this is a good recipe to use when you run out. It is best used with paper. Suitable for all ages with supervision while using a hot stove.

Glue

- ³/₄ cup water
- 2 tablespoons corn syrup
- 1 teaspoon white vinegar*
- ³/₄ cup cold water
- ½ cup cornstarch

Mix the water, corn syrup, and vinegar in a saucepan. Bring to a rolling boil. In a small bowl, mix the cornstarch and cold water. Slowly add this mixture to the first mixture, stirring constantly. Let it stand overnight before using.

* Do not ingest.

Creative Craft Projects Using Paste and Glue

Collage

For use with collage glue

Make collages using magazine pictures, newspapers, or old greeting cards—and so much more. Listed below are some ideas for different collages you can make.

1. Texture collage: Use fabric, fake fur, sandpaper, cotton balls, and cork to make a collage.

2. Scent collage: Use the scratch-and-sniff paint from the previous chapter for this collage. Dab some paint with different scents onto small pieces of paper and glue these to a large piece of paper.

3. Color collage: Tear pieces of colored tissue paper, streamers, or paper.

4. Shape collage: Cut paper into various shapes and glue on paper.

5. Alphabet or number collage: Cut out letters or numbers from magazines and glue onto large piece of paper.

6. Nature collage: Use bark, pebbles, flowers, dirt, and leaves.

7. Themed collage: Use old magazines to find pictures of animals, people, tools, food, or any other themes and glue the pictures onto paper.

Paper sack puppets

Draw eyes, a nose, and a mouth to the bottom flap of a small paper sack. Glue on yarn for hair, or add arms or ears.

Photo frame

Make a square frame using four craft or Popsicle sticks. Glue them together and embellish with any small objects or decorations. Glue yarn to the back for hanging.

Mosaic

Draw any open pattern onto a piece of paper. Tear very small pieces of different colored construction paper and glue these to the inside of the pattern.

Yarn/string picture

Dip a piece of yarn or string into glue and press it onto paper in any design. You can also have the children trace their names, letters, or numbers with the yarn or string.

Yarn hanging

Soak a piece of yarn or string in waterproof glue. Lay it on a piece of waxed paper in a pleasing design. When it dries, peel it from the waxed paper and hang.

Snow globe

For use with waterproof glue

Glue a holiday ornament or any small winter holiday knickknack to the lid of a baby food jar that has had its label removed. Fill jar ³/₄ full with water and add small bits of foil or store-bought artificial snow. Coat the inside of the lid with the same glue, and secure.

Glue earth

For use with glue

Spray any round plastic lid with cooking spray. Coat the surface of the lid with a thick layer of glue. Add 2–3 drops of blue and green food coloring and swirl around with a toothpick so that it looks like the planet Earth. Let dry. Peel from lid.

Suncatchers

For use with glue

Spread the glue onto a plastic lid. Allow to dry and color with markers or paint. Peel away to create neat suncatchers.

Decoupage

For use with collage glue

Cut out pictures from any source. The thinner the paper, the better, but you can also use wallpaper. Spread a layer of glue onto the back of each picture and use them to decorate furniture, plain cardboard boxes, or jars. Then coat the top surface with a thin layer of glue to seal it in. This glue dries non-sticky.

Goop & Glop

5

You can . . .

- stretch and pull it into various shapes
- pour it into various containers
- squeeze it through objects with holes
- press stencils into it and watch it ooze
- add objects to it for decoration and allow to air-dry

Children will be . . .

- using language to describe look and feel
- learning science through experimentation
- developing their senses
- learning math by measuring
- enhancing their fine motor skills
- learning science by discussing physical properties
- predicting and comparing
- practicing science through observation

This is easy to make and children love it. You will need to add starch if the mixture gets too sticky. The more it is manipulated, the more often starch will need to be added. Suitable for ages 3 and up due to the use of liquid starch. Use caution and make sure children do not ingest it.

Wacky Putty

- 1 part white school glue*
- 1 part liquid starch*
- 2–3 drops food coloring

Stir the ingredients together with a spoon, and then with your hands. Add more starch if the mixture is too sticky.

* Do not ingest.

This recipe makes for slimy, messy fun. It's great for toddlers. Suitable for all ages.

Cool Goop

- 1 part salt
- 1 part flour
- 1 part water
- 2–3 drops food coloring (optional)

Mix the ingredients together until smooth. Add food coloring if desired.

This recipe is similar to cool goop, but it's slightly thicker. It's great for young children and is suitable for all ages.

Glop

- 2 cups salt
- $2/3$ cup cold water
- 1 cup cornstarch
- $1/2$ cup cold water

Heat the salt and $2/3$ cup water over low heat until almost boiling. In a separate bowl, mix together cornstarch and $1/2$ cup cold water. Add the cornstarch mixture to the salt mixture and stir thoroughly.

This recipe is great for asking the question: Is it liquid or solid? Suitable for all ages.

Oobleck

- ½ cup cornstarch
- ¼ cup water
- 2–3 drops food coloring

Mix together the cornstarch and water on a cookie sheet that has a small edge around it. Add a drop or two of food coloring. The mixture will be somewhat thick and just barely smooth.

This recipe produces pure sliminess! Use an apron and avoid contact with clothing or other fabrics. Suitable for ages 4 and up with supervision because of the use of borax. Use caution and make sure the children do not ingest. If skin irritation develops from the use of the borax, discontinue use.

Gak

- 1 cup white school glue*
- 3/4 cup water
- 1 tablespoon liquid tempera paint*
- 1/2 teaspoon borax*
- 1/3 cup water

Mix the glue, 3/4 cup water, and paint together with a whisk. Mix 1/3 cup water and 1/2 teaspoon borax in a separate bowl. Slowly add the borax mixture to the glue mixture. Let it stand for about a minute and knead the mixture with your hands. Pour off any remaining liquid. Store in a plastic bag.

* Do not ingest.

This recipe produces a fun rainbow effect. Young children are fascinated with the changing colors of the stew. It's great for toddlers and there's no mess involved. Suitable for all ages.

Rainbow Stew

- ⅓ cup sugar
- 1 cup cornstarch
- 4 cups cold water
- 2–3 drops food coloring

Mix everything but the food coloring together. Heat on the stove until thick. When it is cool, put it in sealable plastic baggies. Add different colors of food coloring and squish it around for a rainbow of colors.

Add this goo to a squeeze bottle and drizzle onto paper.
Suitable for children of all ages.

Drizzle Goo

- 1 cup flour
- 1/4 cup sugar
- 1/4 cup salt
- 3/4 cup water
- 2–3 drops food coloring

Mix all the ingredients together and put in a squeeze bottle. Drizzle onto paper. Allow 2–3 days to dry.

Creative Craft Projects Using Goop and Glop

Recycled container beautification
For use with cool goop or glop

This project can be used to beautify any old container you may have. Spread the goop or glop onto the outside of a container such as a box or a can. You can press objects into it while it is still wet and allow to dry. You can also let the goop or glop on the container air-dry first and then paint it. If you want a thicker coating, allow one layer to dry, and then add another.

Fun with drizzle goo and clay
For use with drizzle goo

Use the drizzle goo recipe to decorate any of the playdoughs or clays in this book to add color and depth.

Spin art
For use with drizzle goo

Punch a hole into the center of a piece of construction paper. Place the paper on an old record player, or place your finger over the hole and use your other hand to spin the paper around. As the paper turns, squeeze the drizzle goo onto the paper.

Other Recipes

6

You can . . .

- use the bubbles to make bubble sculptures, play bubble games, freeze a bubble, or make different colored bubbles
- use wet chalk on dry paper or dry chalk on wet paper, or make chalk shaving pictures
- make mobiles, jewelry, bowls, and vases with papier-mâché
- make layered sand jars, build sand castles, or make casts using the plaster and colored sand
- make your own greeting card or stationery with homemade paper
- dye white yarn or tie-dye a T-shirt
- string colored pasta on yarn to make jewelry, or make macaroni or rice pictures
- make soap, bath salts, perfume, soap crayons, bath oil soak, milk bath, pomander, suncatchers, and art gems and give them away as gifts

Children will be . . .

- learning language and literacy by following along as you read the recipe or by talking about why it was made and for whom
- learning math by naming colors and shapes, reproducing patterns, and seriating
- learning science by observing the changes in the ingredients, discussing how the recipes were made, and mixing together different colors

This recipe makes great bubbles for blowing. Add food coloring to make colored bubbles. Suitable for all ages with supervision. Take care to keep the bubble solution out of eyes.

Bubble Recipe

- 2 cups water
- 1 cup liquid dish soap*
- 2 tablespoons corn syrup
- pipe cleaners

Mix all ingredients together. Shake before use to avoid settling. Use pipe cleaners bent into various shapes to blow bubbles!

* Do not ingest.

This is another great bubble recipe. Try using different materials to form bubbles, such as coat hangers, fly swatters, or strawberry baskets. Suitable for all ages with supervision.

Another Bubble Recipe

- 3 cups water
- 1 cup liquid soap* (baby shampoo or baby bath)
- 1 tablespoon sugar

Mix all the ingredients together.

* Do not ingest.

This chalk is great for creating sidewalk drawings or for writing on chalkboards. Try using wet chalk on dry paper or dry chalk on wet paper for something a little different. Suitable for ages 3 and up, but young children may need help with some of the steps.

Sidewalk Chalk

- 1/2 cup water
- 3 tablespoons plaster of paris*
- 2–3 sprinkles powdered tempera paint,* or as desired

Mix the water and plaster of paris together. Create different colors using the paint, and pour into paper cups. Air-dry approximately 1 hour. Peel away from the cup.

* Do not ingest.

Papier-mâché recipes are great for making piñatas. You can also cover bottles or plastic jars with papier-mâché to make a vase. See the craft projects at the end of this chapter for other great ideas. Suitable for ages 3 and up due to the use of liquid starch. Be careful that the children do not ingest it.

Papier-Mâché

- 2 cups liquid starch,* or as needed
- 2 cups water, or as needed
- newspaper strips

Mix equal parts starch and water. Stir until starch is dissolved. Soak newspaper strips in liquid mixture and pat into place.

* Do not ingest.

Unlike the previous recipe using liquid starch, this recipe contains simple ingredients you probably already have in your kitchen. It's best used for making piñatas. Nontoxic and suitable for all ages with supervision around boiling water.

Another Papier-Mâché

- ½ cup flour
- 2 cups cold water
- 2 cups boiling water
- 3 tablespoons sugar

Combine the flour and cold water in a bowl. Seperately, boil 2 cups of water in a saucepan. Put flour mixture into the saucepan with the boiling water and bring the mixture back to a boil. Remove from the heat and stir in the sugar. Let cool.

This papier-mâché recipe is great for trying out materials other than newspaper for fun new textures. Suitable for all ages with supervision.

Yet Another Papier-Mâché Recipe

- 1 bottle thin paste or white school glue*
- paper napkins, tissue, or toilet paper

Crumple napkins, tissue, or toilet paper and coat with a thin layer of paste or glue. Cover a jar or other container with the paper to make a vase. Must be used immediately. Hardens quickly.

* Do not ingest.

This recipe is a great way to use your leftover dryer lint that you'd otherwise just throw away! This papier-mâché is best used to cover a container such as a jar, box, or bottle. It can also be layered over a balloon to make a piñata. Suitable for all ages with supervision while using the hot stove.

Dryer Lint Papier-Mâché

- 3 cups dryer lint*
- 2 cups water
- $^2/_3$ cup flour

Mix the water and lint together in a large saucepan, stirring well. Slowly add the flour, mixing well. Cook over medium heat, stirring constantly until the mixture holds together, forming peaks. Cover any object with the papier-mâché, and allow to dry 4–5 days.

* Do not ingest.

This is a great recipe for toddlers to make and use. It resembles meringue (though it is nonedible) and smells great. Pile it onto cardboard or heavy paper for cool 3-D art. Suitable for all ages with supervision.

Whipped Soap Flakes

- 1 cup soap flakes*
- 3/4 cup water

Mix the powder with the water and stir until light and fluffy.

* Do not ingest.

This is the only mud you'll find that's clean and great smelling! Add powdered or liquid tempera paint for a different color, or add glitter for some extra sparkle.

Clean Mud

- 3 rolls toilet paper*
- 2 bars white soap*
- 4 cups warm to hot water

Rip up the toilet paper and put it into a large tub. Grind the bars of soap on a cheese grater and add to the toilet paper. Add warm water to get a consistency of watery mush.

* Do not ingest.

Colored sand can be used in any project in place of glitter. Sprinkle it on glue, or layer it in a clear glass container to make a decorative sand jar. See the projects at the end of this chapter for other ideas. Suitable for all ages with supervision.

Colored Sand

- 1 cup fine sand,* or as needed
- powdered tempera paint* as needed

Add the paint to the sand and mix together.

* Do not ingest.

This colored sand recipe can be made with simple food coloring. For easy sprinkling, keep the colored sand in old salt shakers or empty glitter containers. Suitable for all ages with supervision.

Another Colored Sand

- 1 cup fine sand*
- 1 cup water
- 2–3 drops food coloring, or as needed

Fill paper cups half full with sand. Add water to the cups until the sand is completely covered. Add a few drops of food coloring. Stir the mixture together with a plastic spoon and let it set for about 5 minutes. Pour off the water and spoon the sand onto a paper towel. Spread out evenly to dry.

* Do not ingest.

This project takes time, but making your own paper can be very rewarding. Use this recipe to make stationery or your own custom greeting cards. Suitable for ages 5 and up. SUPERVISION IS REQUIRED.

Homemade Paper

- 10 sheets newspaper
- 2 cups water
- 2 tablespoons lint starch*
- piece of screen approximately 5 x 10 inches
- additional newspaper for binding

Tear the 10 sheets of newspaper into very small pieces. Place them in a large pot. Pour in the water and let the mixture sit for a few hours, until the paper is soggy. Blend the water and the soggy paper in a blender, or mix them thoroughly with an egg beater or spoon. The mixture should have the consistency of oatmeal. Pour the mixture into a pan and add lint starch. Stir for about 3 minutes. Dip the screen into the pulp mixture and move the screen around until the pulp covers one half of the screen. You can also spread handfuls of pulp onto the screen directly. The pulp should be about $1/8$-inch thick. Lift the screen

(continued)

out carefully. Hold it level and let it drain for about one minute. Fold the other half of the screen over the pulp and place it on several layers of newspaper. Put more newspaper on the top. Roll a rolling pin or jar over the newspaper to squeeze out the rest of the water. Take off the top newspaper. Remove the pulp carefully from the folded screen.

This will be your paper! Allow the recycled paper to dry overnight before you write on it.

* Do not ingest.

Here's a great way to use all those broken crayons! Make these crayons into any shape you want using an oven mold. Suitable for all ages with supervision while using the oven.

Recycled Crayons

- nonstick oven mold
- peeled crayons in a variety of colors

Preheat the oven to 250 degrees. Place 6–7 peeled crayons into the oven mold, depending on the size of the mold. You can use a variety of colors, or use all of the same color. Place the mold in the oven until the crayons have melted. Turn off the oven and when the oven is completely cool, remove the pan. Push on the bottom of the mold and the crayons will pop out.

* Do not ingest.

These crystals can be used to decorate the pinch pots, bowls, and vases you made in previous recipes. Suitable for all ages with supervision while using the Epsom salt.

Colored Crystals

- 1 tablespoon Epsom salt*
- 1 tablespoon water
- ¼ teaspoon food coloring

Mix the salt and water in a baby food jar. Stir in the food coloring. Observe over the next few days as the water evaporates and small crystals begin to form. For best results, avoid using yellow food coloring.

* Do not ingest.

This recipe can be used to dye paper and cloth. Experiment with different fruits and vegetables to get different colors. Suitable for all ages with supervision while using the hot stove.

Natural Dyes

Boil any of the natural ingredients listed below in water. You can use a single ingredient or mix two or three together to make a new color. When the water is cool, pour it into small containers. Dip small squares of white fabric into the dyes. To tie-dye the fabric, wrap rubber bands around the squares.

Red: red onion skins
Red violet: beets
Pink: cranberries
Yellow: yellow onion skins
Blue: blueberries or blackberries
Green: spinach leaves
Brown: coffee

You can use this recipe for a variety of different activities and crafts. String the macaroni onto a desired length of yarn to make jewelry, or use it to decorate flower pots or picture frames. Glue the rice onto a piece of paper to make a colorful design. Suitable for ages 5 and up. SUPERVISION IS REQUIRED due to use of rubbing alcohol. Use this recipe in a well-ventilated room.

Colored Rice or Macaroni

- 1 cup rice or macaroni noodles
- 1 cup rubbing alcohol*
- 7–8 drops food coloring, or as needed
- acrylic paint* (optional)

Use one plastic bag or bowl for each color you want to make. Place the desired amount of rice or noodles in the bag or bowl. Pour in enough rubbing alcohol so that the rice or noodles are covered. Add a generous amount of food coloring to each container, and let them sit until the rice or noodles become the desired color. This may take several hours. The longer the rice or noodles sit, the brighter the color. Once the rice or noodles reach the desired color, remove them and lay them on a single layer of paper towels to dry. You can use acrylic paints and a paintbrush to handpaint small designs on larger noodles.

* Do not ingest.

Recycle those leftover slivers of bar soap! This recipe is suitable for ages 3 and up due to the use of glycerin. Make sure that it is not ingested, and take care when using the hot stove.

Liquid Soap

- 2 cups soap flakes or grated bar soap*
- ½ gallon water
- 2 tablespoons glycerin*

Mix together all the ingredients in a large pot. Cook over low heat and stir until the soap dissolves. Once the soap has cooled, put it in a jar and cover. Add an extra ½ gallon of water to make a thinner soap.

* Do not ingest.

This recipe makes a great gift. Add essential oil or perfume to make a nice scented soap. Place several soap balls in a square of tulle and tie with a bow. Suitable for all ages with supervision.

Soap Balls

- 2 cups soap flakes*
- $1/4$ cup water
- food coloring, perfume,* or essential oil* as desired

In a bowl, mix the soap flakes and water together and squeeze them between your fingers until well mixed. The mixture should be stiff. Add food coloring, perfumes, or essential oils. Roll into balls, and let the balls air-dry for at least 24 hours before using.

* Do not ingest.

Young children and toddlers can make a lovely perfume for someone special in their lives. Use lavender, rose, honeysuckle, or any other fragrant flower. Suitable for all ages.

Homemade Perfume

- fragrant flower petals
- 1 cup water

Tear the flower petals into small pieces and mix with a little water. Stir until the water turns a light yellow. Pour the mixture into a sealed container. Allow the perfume to sit for a few days before using.

These bath salts make a great gift. Suitable for ages 3 and up, with supervision due to the Epsom salts.

Homemade Bath Salts

- 2½ pounds Epsom salt*
- 3–4 drops food coloring, or as needed
- 2–3 drops perfume,* or as desired

Combine the salt, food coloring, and perfume in a bowl. Mix so that the color is even. Pour into bath salt jars and let stand 4–6 weeks before using.

* Do not ingest.

You can use these crayons to draw on the shower walls and tub. They wash right off! Suitable for all ages with supervision.

Soap Crayons

- 1 cup soap flakes*
- 2 tablespoons hot water
- 2–3 drops food coloring

Put the soap flakes in a bowl and pour the hot water onto the flakes, stirring constantly. The mixture will be hard to stir. Spoon it into small bowls, with one bowl per color. Add food coloring by drops and mix until soap has the consistency of thick paste. Press the soap into molds or ice cube trays. Set it in a dry place to harden. The soap takes about 1 week to dry. After 1 week, remove the soap crayons from the molds and allow a few more days to dry before using.

* Do not ingest.

This recipe leaves your skin feeling soft and smelling great.
Give it away as a gift, or give the children a relaxing bath in it.
Suitable for all ages with supervision while using the stove.

Crème Bath Oil Soak

- 2 tablespoons melted butter
- 1/4 cup + 1 teaspoon corn oil
- 3 whole eggs
- 1/2 cup yogurt
- 1/4 cup + 1 teaspoon witch hazel*
- 1 teaspoon cider
- 1 cup peach or apricot juice
- 1 3/4 cup milk, divided

Melt the butter and mix it with the corn oil. Let stand 1 hour. Mix in
the eggs, stirring gently. Pour this mixture into a blender and add all
the other ingredients, one at a time, adding 1 cup of milk last. Beat at a
low speed. Turn off blender and add the last 3/4 cup of milk, unbeaten.
Shake and add 1/2 cup to your tub. Can be stored up to 1 week in the
refrigerator.

* Do not ingest.

This recipe makes for another relaxing bath soak. Suitable for all ages with supervision.

Milk Bath

- 1 cup powdered milk
- 1 cup baking soda
- 2 tablespoons cornstarch
- 1 tablespoon cream of tartar
- 15–20 drops essential oil*

Mix all the ingredients in a bowl. Store the mixture in an airtight container. Add ½ cup to your bath and enjoy!

* Do not ingest.

Make holiday and seasonal window decorations with this recipe. Decorate them using glitter, small flowers, leaves, or any other small, decorative item. Suitable for all ages with supervision.

Window Clings and Suncatchers

- 1/2 cup white school glue*
- 2–3 drops food coloring
- transparency sheets or other clear film
- patterns
- glitter* or small flowers

Add a few drops of food coloring into the glue bottle and mix well. With a pencil draw a pattern on a piece of paper and put the design under the clear film or transparency. Trace over the lines with the glue, making sure all of the lines are connected. Fill in the design with different colors of glue, if desired. Let dry for 12 hours. Peel off and place on any glass surface. To store, place between sheets of plastic wrap.

To make suncatchers, pour a thin layer of the colored glue into a plastic lid, filling it halfway to the top. Add small decorative items such as glitter, shaped confetti, or small pieces of torn tissue paper. Allow 2–4 days to dry, and then pop it out of the lid and hang.

* Do not ingest.

Use these beautiful art gems to decorate some of your dough and clay creations. Add them to the bead clay to embellish your beaded jewelry. Avoid getting these gems wet or they'll melt! Suitable for ages 3 and up due to the use of rubbing alcohol. Use this recipe in a well-ventilated room.

Art Gems

- ½ cup rock salt*
- ¼ cup rubbing alcohol*
- 2–3 drops food coloring

Mix all the ingredients together. Red, yellow, and blue food coloring make beautiful "gems" for art activities. You can also mix equal parts of each color to make brown for small "rocks."

* Do not ingest.

This recipe is a great way to add a nice flower pattern to different materials. Make imprints on shirts, paper, pillowcases, placemats, and more! Suitable for all ages with supervision.

Flower Transfers

- fresh flowers
- rubber mallet
- plastic wrap
- fabric or article of clothing

Place flowers facedown on the fabric. Cover with a layer of clear plastic wrap. Gently tap flowers using rubber mallet. Remove the plastic wrap and flowers.

Use this to clean any copper object. It's a fun science experiment! Suitable for all ages with supervision while using the vinegar.

Penny Cleaner

- ½ cup vinegar*
- 2 tablespoons salt
- penny

Fill a cup halfway with vinegar. Add the salt, and drop in a penny. Watch how it changes.

* Do not ingest.

Creative Craft Projects Using Bubbles

Make bubbles using different blowers

For use with any bubble recipe

Use a variety of materials to blow your bubbles. Try pipe cleaners bent into different shapes, fly swatters, strawberry baskets, coat hangers, strainers, funnels, potato mashers, or anything else you can think of.

Colored bubble print

For use with any bubble recipe

Add a drop or two of food coloring to the bubble solution to make colored bubbles. Blow your bubbles onto a piece of white paper. When they pop, they leave a neat design behind!

Colored bubble print #2

For use with any bubble recipe

Pour the bubble solution into several small pie pans. Add a drop or two of food coloring to each pan, using one color per pan. Using a straw, blow bubbles until the pan is full of them. Lay a white piece of paper onto the bubbles. Sit back and wait. The bubbles will pop a design onto the paper. Lift paper from the bubbles. Place it on a different pan for layers of colors, or just keep it one color.

Creative Craft Projects Using Sidewalk Chalk

Texture rubbings

Place any flat object that has a pattern or texture under a piece of typing paper. Rub chalk over the object. Spray the paper with hair spray to set the chalk.

Wet and dry

Draw a design using wet chalk on dry paper or dry chalk on wet paper.

Tricycle roads

Use sidewalk chalk to draw pretend roads on the sidewalk for children to ride their tricycles on. Add pedestrian crosswalks too! You can also make roads for toy cars!

Positive/negative design

Cover an entire piece of white paper with a heavy layer of colored chalk. Using a black crayon, color heavily over the chalk. Place a second piece of white paper on top of the colored paper. Draw any design on top of this paper using a pencil. Make sure to press hard. Remove the paper, and you'll have a nice pattern on the bottom paper.

Sandpaper writing

Using the chalk, draw a picture on fine sandpaper. Seal the picture with a thin coat of hair spray.

Chalk float design

Grate a piece of chalk into a shallow pan of water. The chalk will float on top of the water. Carefully lay a piece of white paper on top of the chalk. The chalk will be absorbed by the paper, creating an interesting design.

Creative Craft Projects Using Papier-Mâché

Papier-Mâché containers

For use with any of the papier-mâché recipes in this book

For this project, you will be making containers out of papier-mâché to store small objects. Lightly grease a small plastic bowl, vase, cup, or whatever shape you want your container to be. Add layers of papier-mâché to the surface. Allow it to dry at least 24 hours before adding more layers. Dry completely and carefully slip off the form.

Piñata

For use with any of the papier-mâché recipes in this book

Layer papier-mâché onto a blown-up balloon. Add several layers of papier-mâché, allowing it to dry between layers. Carefully cut a hole into the top for the candy. Paint or cover with tissue paper.

Vase

For use with any of the papier-mâché recipes in this book. Dryer lint papier-mâché works especially well.

Layer the papier-mâché over a plastic soda bottle. When dry, slowly slide it off the bottle. Leave it looking natural or paint it when completely dry.

Creative Craft Projects Using Whipped Soap Flakes

Winter wreath

Cut an inner and outer circle out of a piece of stiff cardboard to make a wreath form. Pile the whipped soap flakes onto the form and press in winter items (pine cones, leaves, acorns, etc.). Make a holiday wreath by adding ribbon, plastic candy canes, etc. Allow to dry.

Colored snow

Use 2–3 drops of food coloring to add color to the soap flakes.

Diorama

Lay a shoebox on its side. Add a thick layer of whipped soap flakes to the bottom, and form hills and valleys to create a winter scene. Add small plastic figures or other items before it dries, if you desire.

Creative Craft Projects Using Colored Sand

Color shakers
For use with any colored sand

Keep your different colors of sand separated in salt shakers. You can use these to sprinkle the sand on designs you make with glue, just as you would glitter.

Sand jars
For use with any colored sand

Spread a layer of colored sand in a jar. Continue adding various colored layers until you reach the top.

Creative Craft Projects Using Homemade Paper

Stationery

Use this recipe to make custom stationery. Decorate it with stamps, stickers, or anything else you can think of.

Greeting cards

Use this paper to create unique and custom-made greeting cards. For a wintery look, spread collage glue over the card cover and sprinkle it with sugar.

Creative Craft Projects Using Colored Crystals or Art Gems

Decorative elements
For use with art gems or colored crystals

Either of these crafts can be glued onto a variety of objects to add a special sparkle.

Gem beads
For use with art gems

Press art gems into the clay beads from chapter 2 before drying.

Decorate pottery
For use with art gems

Press the art gems into pinch pots, clay vases, or clay bowls before drying.

Decorate a picture frame
For use with art gems
Requires adult supervision

Add art gems to a plain wooden photo frame using hot glue.

Recycled boxes

For use with art gems

Glue the art gems onto a recycled box for a pretty organizer.

Decorate a vase

For use with colored crystals or art gems

Add the colored crystals or art gems to a clear jar or bottle. Insert a sprig of silk flowers.

Creative Craft Projects Using Recycled Crayons

Crayon rubbings

Make rubbings of cardboard, bark, sandpaper, coins, leaves, etc., by placing them under a sheet of paper and rubbing a crayon over the paper. Use anything that has some kind of texture to it.

Crayon resist

Draw a picture using crayon on paper. Brush a layer of paint over entire picture. The crayon will resist the paint.

Melted crayon on fabric

Requires adult supervision

Color a picture on a small piece of cotton fabric, such as a T-shirt or a swatch of cloth. Place the fabric facedown on a layer of newspaper, and cover with a damp cloth and another layer of newspaper. Slide a hot iron back and forth over the newspaper a few times. The color will now be imprinted on the fabric. Use this project to decorate T-shirts or to make pillows, potholders, or anything else that involves fabric. Do not dry these items in a dryer after washing or the crayon will melt. Hang dry only.

Melted crayon on paper
Requires adult supervision

Peel the paper off crayons. Using a grater, shave the crayons into piles. Sprinkle the crayon shavings onto a piece of paper and add another sheet of paper on top or fold the paper over. Slide an iron set on low heat back and forth over the paper until the crayon is melted. Open or remove the paper for a fun design!

Scratch art

Cover an entire piece of paper with a thick layer of crayon. Scratch a design into the crayon drawing using a toothpick.

Rainbow crayon

Add several different colored crayons to one mold and melt in the oven to form a neat rainbow crayon!

Sparkle picture

Draw a picture with crayon on black construction paper. Paint the entire paper with a mixture of salt and water.

Creative Craft Projects Using Colored Macaroni or Rice

Trinket box

Spread a thick layer of glue onto a small, plain cardboard box. Press the colored pasta or rice into the glue. You can also add colored sand, glitter, art gems, or colored crystals for additional decoration. Use these cute boxes for giving gifts, such as soap balls or soap crayons.

Decorative jar lids

Spread glue on the top of a jar lid. Press colored pasta, rice, art gems, etc., into the glue. You can use these decorative jars to hold some of the other recipe creations in this book, such as the bath salts, perfume, or bath soaks, and give them as gifts!

Pasta or rice pattern

Draw a simple line drawing or write your child's name onto paper. Follow the lines with glue and add pasta or rice.

Pasta jewelry

Use any pasta that has a hole in the center. String yarn or ribbon through the pasta to make bracelets and necklaces.

Creative Craft Projects Using Window Clings and Suncatchers

Stained glass suncatchers

Spread glue into desired plastic form. Add food coloring. To create a suncatcher using multiple colors, use a craft stick to stir in the glue and keep the colors away from one another. When you have decorated it to your pleasing, allow to dry.

Glitter clings

Use the window cling recipe. While glue is still wet, sprinkle on glitter or colored sand.

Color blobs

Add a bit of liquid tempera paint to the glue recipe from chapter 4. Drop a small amount of the mixture onto waxed paper using craft sticks or a spoon. When they have dried, peel them off. You can use them to decorate the windows, but you can also glue them onto paper and paint around them.

Discovery Bottles

7

Discovery bottles are an easy and inexpensive item that children love! They provide for a great cognitive activity that promotes children's thinking skills and encourages the use of their imagination. You can add many different things to these bottles to correspond to whatever theme you are studying or to any holiday. They can be used to discuss scientific concepts and math skills, and they also make a great quiet-time activity. You can use large or small plastic bottles, but smaller ones work best for little hands. Discovery bottles are easy to make. Simply follow the instructions below! Suitable for all ages.

1. Find an empty, clean plastic soda bottle.
2. Remove the label.
3. Add any of the items listed in the following projects to the bottle.
4. Seal the bottle with hot glue.
5. Have fun!

Alphabet Bottle

Write a letter of the alphabet on the outside of the bottle and fill the bottle with small objects that begin with that letter.

Beach Bottle

Fill the bottle half full with sand and add shells, pebbles, plastic sea creatures, etc.

Bubble Bottle

Fill the bottle 3/4 full with water. Add liquid dish soap until full. Shake for the bubbles. You can also add food coloring to create colored bubbles.

Crayon Shaving Bottle

Fill the bottle 2/3 full with crayon shavings. Add water.

Desert Bottle

Fill the bottle 2/3 full with sand. Add small plastic snakes or lizards.

Dirt Bottle

Add soil to a bottle and fill the rest of the bottle with water. Shake to see what happens.

Estimation Bottle

Fill the bottle with a certain number of beans or other small objects. Have the children estimate how many are in the bottle.

Fish Tank Bottle

Fill the bottle 1/4 full with water. Add a few drops of blue food coloring and a drop of liquid detergent. Add a small amount of sand or aquarium gravel. Blow up 2 small balloons, releasing most of the air. These will be the fish. Tie the end closed and push into the bottle. NOTE: Keep the balloons out of the hands of children.

Float Bottle

Fill the bottle 1/2 full with water. Add any items that float.

Glitter Bottle

Fill bottle 2/3 full with glitter. Add water. Shake.

Glow-in-the-Dark Bottle

Add small glow-in-the-dark items to the bottle.

Holiday Bottle

Fill a bottle 2/3 full with water, and add small plastic holiday-related items, glitter, etc. You can also add food coloring to the bottle according to the holiday.

Lava Lamp Bottle

Fill the bottle nearly to the top with cooking oil. Add a lot of food coloring. Adding more than one color will result in black bubbles. Seal the bottle tightly.

Magnet Bottle #1

Fill the bottle with magnetic and nonmagnetic items. Attach a magnetic wand with yarn to the bottle. Rub the magnet against the side of the bottle to see which objects are magnetic and which aren't.

Magnet Bottle #2

Add magnetic objects to a bottle and fill the bottom with sand. Attach a magnetic wand with yarn to the bottle. Rub the magnet against the side of the bottle to find out what is hiding in the sand.

Marble Bottle

Fill the bottle with transparent hair gel or shampoo. Add a marble. Turn the bottle upside down and see how the marble moves.

Mystery Bottle

Cover the bottle with black construction paper. Place a noisy object inside, and have children guess what is inside the bottle.

Number Bottle

Write a number on the outside of the bottle and fill it with the number of objects you write on the outside.

Quiet Bottle

Add paper scraps, cotton balls, and tissue to the bottle.

Rain Bottle

Fill the bottle with a box of toothpicks. Add uncooked rice, leaving a $1\frac{1}{2}$ inch empty space at the top. When the rice falls through the toothpicks, it sounds like rain.

Sand Bottle

Fill the bottom of the bottle with sand. Add water. Shake it to see what happens. You can also add food coloring to the sand and water for a different look.

Seasonal Bottle

Fill the bottle with seasonal items.

Sink Bottle

Add items to the bottle that will sink in water. Fill the bottle $\frac{1}{2}$ full with water.

Snow or Ice Bottle

Fill the bottle half full with snow or ice. Record what happens over the next few hours.

Sprout Bottle

Add a piece of wet sponge to the bottle. Sprinkle grass seed on the sponge. Observe what happens over the next days or weeks.

Static Bottle

Place Styrofoam pieces in the bottle. Rub on your hair.

Syrup Bottle

Add metallic confetti or glitter to the bottle. Fill the bottle with corn syrup. Gently turn the bottle back and forth.

Tornado Bottle

Roll pieces of foil into balls and place in the bottle. Fill the remaining part of the bottle with water so that it is almost full. Add a small drop of detergent.

Wave Bottle

Fill half of the bottle with either cooking oil or baby oil. Then add water so that the bottle is 3/4 full. Add blue food coloring. Put some seashells in the bottle too, if you'd like!

Discovery
Table Ideas

8

The discovery table is a wonderful place for children to play. In a child care setting, the discovery table usually consists of a table with raised sides that contains sand, water, corn starch, or other materials children can explore and manipulate. Unfortunately, too often teachers put only water and sand in the discovery table. Why limit the children to only two options? There are a multitude of materials that can be placed here. The possibilities are endless!

If you are a parent or family child care provider and don't have a discovery table at home, you can make your own by simply using a rubber tub and adding any materials you want. Let your child dig in and play!

Many of the recipes in this book can be used in a discovery table. Placing shaving cream, paint, clean mud, or goop in this area gives children something different to play with. In "Beyond Sand and Water" I have included numerous such ideas.

In "Discovery Table Add-Ons" you will find props that you can add to the sand and water play. The children will enjoy playing, pouring, and measuring with these. There is also a list of seasonal items that can be placed in this area for each month of the year. Experiment with these ideas or add your own! Children always enjoy finding something new in the discovery table or tub.

Let's get started!

Beyond Sand and Water

There are many wonderful items that can be placed in the discovery table or tub instead of sand and water. Let this be a starting point! Use your imagination and come up with other items. Don't forget, most of the craft recipe creations can be added to the discovery table too!

NOTE: Many of these items are small and should not be used by children under 3 years of age. Supervise children well while playing.

aquarium stones
beads
beans
birdseed
bolts and screws
buttons
cards
coffee grounds
colored rice/noodles
confetti
cornmeal
cornstarch and water
cotton balls
craft store feathers
dried corn
dry cereal

felt pieces
flour
flowers and dirt
foam packing peanuts
foil
grass seed
hay or straw
lotion
marbles
material scraps
noodles (wet or dry)
nuts
oatmeal
paint and brushes
paper and scissors
peanut shells

pebbles

Ping-Pong balls

plastic eggs

plastic grass

play money

playdough/clay

popcorn

potato flakes

potpourri

pudding

rice

rock salt

rocks

sandpaper and blocks

sawdust

seashells

shaving cream

shredded paper

spools

Styrofoam pieces

Discovery Table Add-Ons

Add these to sand and water play for new ways of exploring! Many of these items can be interchanged and used in either sand or water. These are just a few suggestions to get your discovery table started!

NOTE: Some of the items listed below are small and should not be used by children under 3 years of age. Supervise children well while playing.

Water Play

aquarium stones	paintbrushes
bark	Ping-Pong balls
boats	pitchers
cars	plastic dolls
clothespins	plastic tubing
corks	rubber gloves
eggbeaters	rubber worms
food coloring	sieves
hoses	slotted spoons
housekeeping toys	small balls
ice cube trays	small plastic toys
ice cubes	soap
ladles	sponges
loofas	spray bottles
margarine tubs	toothbrushes
measuring cups/spoons	turkey basters
medicine droppers	water pump/wheels

Sand Play

aluminum pie pans

buckets

containers (various sizes)

craft sticks

fake flowers

funnels

glitter

gloves

leaves

lids

magnets

magnifying glasses

measuring spoons/cups

muffin tins

pine cones

plastic fruits and vegetables

plastic molds

pots and pans

powdered tempera paint

small rakes

rocks

scoops

shells

shovels

spoons

toy vehicles

twigs

water

whisks

wood/bark

Monthly Discovery Table Ideas Using Creative Craft Recipes

Use the craft ideas from this book to add new sensory experiences to your table or tub every month!

January	Whipped Soap Flakes Clean Mud
February	Playdough/Clay, colored red or pink Salt Dough
March	Cool Goop, colored green Clean Mud
April	Rainbow Stew Herbal Clay
May	Potpourri Dough Homemade Bath Salts Soap Crayons

| June | Sun Clay |
| | Bubble Recipe |

| July | Sand Clay |
| | Colored Sand |

August	Nature's Playdough
	Colored Macaroni or Rice
	Bubble Recipe

| September | Bathtub Fingerpaint |

| October | Bumpy Texture Dough |
| | Glop |

November	Bread Clay
	Pumpkin Pie Spice Dough
	(see Gingerbread Dough)

| December | Cinnamon Dough |
| | Gingerbread Dough |